MW01292834

Intentional Living

How to Not Die with Regrets by Living a Life That Matters

A 3-Step Blueprint

By Simeon Lindstrom

Table of Contents

Introduction

Some time ago, I stumbled across this quote – and felt as though it had slapped me across the face.

Like any thirty-something, questions of my own mortality had gradually changed from being an interesting hypothetical to something very real, and very scary. While the first part of my life had seem filled with new beginnings and first times, the second half looked a bit more dire: I was beginning to realize that there would be *last times* for everything, too. And like the typical thirty-something, I had a mild existential crisis about it: had I really lived my life well up until that moment? Had I wasted my youth, and was I possibly wasting my life right this minute?

When I saw this quote, it dawned on me: I wasn't actually afraid of death itself. How could I be? After all, I wouldn't be around when it happened. Rather, what I was afraid of was the crushing awareness that I wasn't living while I actually had the chance.

I looked back on my twenties and sadly realized that they were finished. I would never be in my twenties again. Life moved only forward, and the choices I had made during those years were already made, and could never be changed. In a way, it was the death of that part of my life. Was I happy with it, looking back? Did I have regrets?

I didn't know what my future looked like, but I knew that I didn't want to have that same feeling when I'd be very old and looking back on the whole of my life. I didn't want that sinking sense that I could have done more, and that there was still some life in me left unlived, some doors I had left unopened, some questions I had left unanswered. Something seemed deeply horrifying about the idea of leaving this world, thinking, "No, wait! I'm not done yet!"

And so I got to thinking about how to *not* do that, and my questions led me to writing this book. In these pages, I want to share the three key strategies that I have used to cultivate a life that, at the end of the day, actually matters.

I've learnt a lot on my journey to clearing away the rubbish and honing in on what's important. I've learnt that disappointment and self-doubt is at the root of so many people's fear of really *living*. I've learnt that sometimes the only thing holding you back from a life that is fulfilling and deeply meaningful is that you keep telling yourself stories in which you never do. Finally, I've learnt that when it comes to living a life without regrets, it's all about finding, cherishing and creating *value*, in everything you do.

The exercises I've suggested here are borne of my own insights and experience, but they are certainly not authoritative. If you've picked up this book, there's a good chance that your instinct for meaning and value is alive and well within you – trust that instinct. Of course, before making any decisions, I ask that you keep an open mind as you read on.

Ready?

Chapter 1 - The Big Disappointment

When you were little, your parents probably told you that you were a very special, very clever little boy or girl who could do whatever they wanted, and achieve whatever they set their hearts to. And even if they didn't, it's a rare child who isn't completely convinced that the world is an accommodating place which will only support their dreams of becoming a president or an astronaut or a unicorn trainer.

But when was the last time you met an adult who believed something like this? In fact, the implicit understanding is that adulthood is all about moderating your dreams. Reigning your passions in. You come to terms with your limitations, take a few hard knocks and maybe even come to believe that your life is, in the end, insignificant. Have you ever noticed how "grow up!" is used as an insult? It's as though the adult world is intolerant of hopes and dreams that seem too fanciful, or too hopeful.

"The big disappointment" is really a series of tiny, accumulated disappointments. You realize that there is always someone better than you, even at the interests you hold most dear. You become keenly aware that life is not fair, and that others who are no more deserving than you enjoy more resources, more luck, more wealth. With your growing awareness of the complexity of the world around you, your own sphere of influence seems so small and negligible.

How could *you* ever make a difference? How could *your* life ever be meaningful when there are literally billions of other people on this earth?

Like many other people, you may have chosen to forfeit some of your most cherished dreams. You may have sternly told yourself to grow up and pushed away your loftiest and most exciting visions for yourself and your place in the world. You may have grudgingly put your head down and set your mind to more achievable, more "normal" goals, like getting on with a job. Or saving and getting a mortgage. Perhaps you quietly internalized the idea that it's foolish to try to do anything different, and that life is too expensive and unpredictable and scary to risk pursuing something that would be more meaningful to you.

If any of that resonates with you, you'll already know the problem with this approach: it doesn't work. After all, you're here right now, reading this book. No matter how thoroughly we try to forget it, our yearning for a significant, meaningful and valuable life can't just disappear.

That yearning comes out in our dreams, or late at night when we're done with work for the day and we're "free" to imagine a world where things are different. We say "one day" or daydream about having the guts to run away and start over again.

If we've been denying this instinct in ourselves for a long time, it may be second nature to never admit these dreams to anyone else. We think it's normal to work on a novel for months and then hide it in the bottom drawer. We look at successful, fulfilled people and tell ourselves, "well, of course it's easy for them, since they have so much money, influence or luck".

But our "childish" hopes and dreams for something more never really leave us. In fact, *getting older* can be an ironic catalyst for bringing some of those neglected longings out of the woodwork. Have we really done as well as we could have? Will we be able to rest on our deathbed without regrets?

As we begin this book, I want to ask you to take a look at the instinct that drove you to purchase and read it. Try to be as honest as possible: why bother at all?

Your answer to this question will provide some clues about the limitations you may have been putting on yourself thus far – and the key to removing those limitations.

- *"Nothing really made me seek this book out. It's no big deal. I read all sorts of things so reading this means nothing. I know that most self-help books are nonsense so I don't have any great expectations."*

- *"My life is a bit of a mess. Clearly solving the problems of life are too big and difficult for me, so I need guidance."*

- "I don't know. I haven't really thought about it!"

- "I like reading this kind of material – it keeps me aware and engaged with my life goals."

- "If I'm honest, I don't know why I'm reading this – previous self-help books haven't worked, why should this one?"

There's no need to over-analyze your motivations for starting this guide at this point, but just become aware of your attitude going in. Try to be honest and admit if you're embarking from the get-go with an attitude that fully expects to fail. Just notice if you're unconsciously limiting yourself. Will it really cost you anything, to hope that wonderful things lie in store for you...?

Chapter 2 - The 3-Step Plan

For a positive book that is supposed to be all about intentional living, the picture I've painted so far is a pretty grim one! If this were an infomercial, this would be the point where I jump in and tell you all about my amazing product, and how it's precisely what you need to solve all your problems.

But this *isn't* an infomercial, and there are no quick and easy fixes when it comes to the greatest task you'll ever undertake: the art of living well.

The remainder of this book will be structured around three key steps to cultivating and developing a style of life that is intentional and geared towards deep, personal fulfillment. Too many people reach the end of their time on this planet and think "I should have done this or that".

This guide is intended to pre-empt this.

What could you do right here, right now, so that you won't have to say those dreaded words on your deathbed? What could you do right now that will make your future 90-year-old self proud? How can you be and feel and act right now that will not only spare your future self these regrets, but have that version of yourself smiling and thinking, "that was a pretty good life, I'm ready to go now without any fear or sadness"?

Pretty heavy thing to think about, I know, but finding out the answers to these questions is the purpose of the chapters that follow.

The three keys are:

1) Develop deeper intention and self-awareness
2) Take charge of your "stories"
3) Add value for a more valuable life

Each of these steps builds on the other two. We'll consider each of them in turn, but before we do, I want to note a few important things: firstly, the information written here is just that. Information. It's just words on a page, or pixels on a screen. And unless you actively choose to do something with what you read here, they will never be more than that.

I can't stress this enough.

Many people read inspirational material or self-help books and feel like they "don't work". Reading a book about healthy lifestyle and weight loss won't do a thing for you if you keep up with the same bad habits you always had, and reading a book about making changes to your life won't "work" if you don't actively engage with the information once you've closed the book.

Of course, there isn't anything magical in the words written here. And reading about change is not the same as changing. Change, if it happens, will happen *after* you've read and decided to put the ideas in practice. This is why each of the following keys to purposeful living not only has a section of new information, but also a practical way to *apply* that information out in the real world, right now. I've tried to include examples of real people where relevant.

Secondly, although I have given three "steps", the process outlined here is not so much three distinct steps and then you're done and finished forever. Rather, it's a never-ending cycle, one where you constantly learn to improve in increments.

As you read and try some of the suggestions in the book, my hope is you'll start feeling more aware, more in control and more joyful in your life. But that doesn't mean that on the way there you won't experience some bad days, too.

Part of change means breaking down old ways of thinking – and that process of breaking things down can be painful. Part of change is also feeling stuck occasionally, or uninspired ...or even taking a few steps back.

Before we begin, I want to encourage you to be compassionate with yourself. Change takes time. Go slowly, be kind and keep returning to the things that challenge you!

Chapter 3 - Beginning with Intention

Life isn't about finding yourself. It's about creating yourself.

George Bernard Shaw

Let's start with the first key to a life free of regrets: intentional living. What do we even mean when we call something *intentional*?

A clue to the whole point of living intentionally is to consider that another way of saying it is to do something "on purpose". When you act with intention, YOU come to the fore and act as the full human agent that you are. You plan ahead, you commit, and then you act in accordance with that plan to bring about goals that are meaningful to you. You are awake. You are responsible. You are deliberate.

There are immense advantages to this state of mind: a person who acts and chooses consciously is fully present for everything that unfolds in their lives. Because they are proactively choosing their actions and their responses, they have a degree of maturity and control over their fate. When adversity strikes, they can quickly recover and return to thriving.

On the other hand, when you live intentionally, you also sign up for more responsibility. The darker side of taking more control is that you can no longer blame anything or anyone but yourself. In a court of law, people will argue over whether something was accidental or pre-meditated because intention is the root of whether an action is meaningful or not. When you live "on purpose", in other words, you can be judged. You are culpable.

Living intentionally can be frightening, but it is the foundation of a regret-less, meaningful life. This cannot be emphasized enough: *there is no meaning without intention.*

If you walk down the road and find some money, well, nobody intended to leave it there for you to find. It's just luck, and there's no "meaning" to it because it's accidental and purely random. The same can be said for catching a rare disease by chance or winning the lottery. But because there is no *intention* in any of these events, there can be no meaning. Many people live their entire lives this way. What happens just happens. They experience every event as though it were as random and lacking in meaning as finding money on the street by accident.

But what if you are not satisfied to live a life that feels random and meaningless?

Well, then you can act to bring about the things you value, and in so doing, *create* meaning. This requires *intention*. You can actively decide that you will make money rather than hope to find it in the street, and work hard and educate yourself so that you can be financially successful. You can actively choose to live a healthy life to minimize your chances of getting ill.

With a firm intention in place, all your actions can be measured against this yardstick: did you live up to your goals? Instantly, your actions go from being random to being purposeful. You go from being reactive to the events others create, to being proactive, and someone that originates their own events.

But ironically, many self-help books begin with the hidden premise that you are actually *not* in control of your life. They present the equivalent of tips and tricks to finding more money on the street, or tell you to "accept" the things that make you unhappy because a lot of it's just down to luck anyway, right?

They tell you that happiness is something that you need to buy or be part of a special group to enjoy. They tell you that your problems are somebody else's fault and that you should just seek a bit of happiness in the fact that you can't do anything about it. We saw in a previous section that people are urged to succumb to the "grow up" message, which deep down is the message: "give up".

In this book we'll take a different approach: you are in control of your life. Your life *does* have meaning and you can live in a principled, focused, deliberate way that makes your time on this earth significant. You are responsible. You are in charge.

But the very first thing you must do is *decide* for all that to be the case.

Intention Exercise One: Don't Take Anyone's Word for it; Think Critically

I have a friend whose mother told her all the time that she was unintelligent and would never succeed in life. Because she was just a child when she first heard this, she believed it wholeheartedly. She kept on believing it while she sailed through school with high grades, and earned a difficult degree in record time. She believed it as people looked up to her and she became an expert in her field. She even believed it well after her mother passed away and she was surrounded by nothing but praise for her success and intelligence.

Why couldn't my friend see herself as we saw her? As a child, you trust and believe your parents. My friend, as smart as she was, never took the leap to *question* what her mother told her over and over. She took her word for it. She never sat down and asked herself what *she* thought, what *she* wanted. She took her mother's judgment and substituted it for her own.

While she suffered with low self-esteem for years and years, she never had the insight or the intention to create her own identity. Her mother had labeled her, and this was powerful enough to remain even after her mother was long gone.

In this exercise, you're going to try and question your own assumptions – about yourself, others or life in general. Don't even take your *own* word for it! How many people have wasted their lives doing things other people said would make them happy? How much happiness have you talked yourself out of because you believed your own negative self-talk?

To do this exercise, first ask yourself what you *want*.

Not what others tell you you want, not what you wish you wanted. But your deepest, truest and most lasting desires.

Imagine you're in a colossal, magical restaurant and are sitting down, ready to order a new life for yourself. What do you order? Go wild. For now, don't worry about what's practical or correct or fashionable or expected of you. Just go with it.

Do you imagine a colorful, creative existence filled with interesting people and places? A life of service and learning? An adoring family? Dig deep with this, and don't just go with whatever first pops into your head. Ask, would you *really* be happy with a lot of money? Are you too afraid to admit your real desires? Do you feel too ambitious or not ambitious enough? Just go with it.

A psychologist friend tells me that many people come to her complaining that they have achieved everything they were supposed to achieve to make them happy: impressive careers, spouses, children. But they felt deeply unfulfilled anyway. Too late they discover that those were just the things they *thought* they wanted. They had lived so long in borrowed desires that they had forgotten the joy they got from a humble vegetable patch, or that childhood hobby they dropped years ago.

What do you *want*? Not just crave in the moment, but want in a deeper sense?

Now, pick a day and go out into the world to *express* this wish, even if it's in a very small way. In your magical café visualization, maybe you imagined a more social life, where you felt more deeply connected to others. In this case, remember this desire the next time you talk to someone, and talk to them as though you already live in that fantasy life you created. If you pictured a more spiritual life, express this in the way you carry yourself for that day, even if it's just to go to the supermarket or fill your gas tank.

What happens when you begin to put your desires out there? What happens when you say, "This is what I want"?

For just this one day, listen carefully to every bit of information that comes your way and ask, "Is this what I want?" Think critically about what others tell you. Is it true? Is it really true? You can take this exercise as far as you like.

Let's imagine a woman who feels burnt out and uninspired by her life. She works all day and feels like she gets nowhere, she's not appreciated at home and her marriage has lost all its spark. So she chooses a day to ask what she really wants, and to look critically at what passes into her awareness.

She comes home after work and looks at the pile of dishes in the sink. She definitely doesn't want that. She spends an hour preparing a meal that her family seem uninterested in. But she has to feed them, right? She has no choice.

Or does she? When she thinks critically about this, she realizes it isn't necessarily true. While she has been laboring under the idea that everyone in the family wants elaborate daily meals, her included, she's missed something: that her teenaged children and busy husband don't care either way. And neither does she. What she really wants instead is just to sit down, relax and enjoy the evenings with her family rather than slave away at the things social media tells her she wants.

Such a woman doesn't need advice on how to "do it all" or how to prepare gourmet meals in even less time. She just needs to realize that doing so isn't even something she wants in the first place…

Intention Exercise Two: Making the Decision, Setting Your Intention

If you've gone a long time on autopilot, asking these questions can be a bit overwhelming at first. It's easier to default to what's expected instead of taking the time to develop your own intention. Have you ever heard someone talk about marrying their partners just because enough time has passed and it just feels like the thing they *should* do next? But by going along with external expectations for what you should want and value, you avoid asking yourself what *you* want, and why.

You forfeit your chance to make meaning for yourself, and you open the door for regrets.

The next opportunity you have, practice making decisions and flexing those intention muscles. Pick any period of time – an hour, day, or week – and then take a moment to focus in on your intention for that period. A good daily habit is to "set" your intention early every morning, but you could also do it before bed or even with each passing hour.

Find a quiet place to sit, go still inside yourself and focus on your breathing. Take a few moments to become aware of your body and your mind and just notice where you are, without any judgment.

Next, zoom in on the frame of mind you want to carry with you throughout the rest of the hour, day or week. You are not thinking of specific goals here, but rather your ideal attitude. Think of it like tuning an instrument before playing, narrowing the beam of a laser or twiddling the knob on a radio to find just the right channel.

Picture the day ahead, including all its challenges and unexpected events. Now picture yourself facing those challenges, but anchored in the intention that you have already set for yourself. Have fun with visualization, if you like. You might, for example, decide that you want to be accepting and calm of whatever transpires that day, and visualize yourself being cloaked with a shield of light. Or you could set your intention to be strong and assertive, and imagine yourself made of steel and responding to any threats with courage. It's all up to you.

With your intention set, you're aware, awake and in control.

You may be wondering exactly *what* intention you should set, but try not to get too bogged down in doing this exercise "right". I have mentioned being calm or being strong as possible states of mind, but there's no reason that these should appeal to you. In fact, the details of the state of mind you choose don't matter that much; what does matter is that you are aware and *deliberately choosing* that state of mind.

A woman with anger problems may take the time every morning to set her intention for the day: to be calm. She focuses on this and meditates before her morning shower, visualizing herself swimming miles under the sea, in slow motion, perfectly at peace in the deep blue. She knows that no matter how stressful her day gets, she can always close her eyes and be back in that peaceful place again. In time, she realizes that her anger – and every situation – is completely within her control.

As you get more practice asking yourself what you actually want (the first exercise) and then deliberately setting your intention (the second exercise) you will find that awareness of your desires actually grows, and more specific goals will begin to form in your mind by themselves. Eventually, you'll become less and less susceptible to external pressure and more anchored in something that is actually meaningful for you. For now, it's enough to just pause for a moment, and practice taking the reins.

Chapter 4 - The Power of Stories

Before we launch into the next chapter, let's take a moment to consider the previous one. Did you dive in and engage fully? Or did you skim through, assume you understood what was being said and then skip actually doing the exercises? Remember, intellectually comprehending an idea is not the same as *experiencing* it!

Let's move on.

In this chapter, we'll be expanding on some of the ideas from the first. The previous two exercises were all about getting acquainted with your deeper desires and then taking the time to say yes, you *choose* those desires. On the surface, this seems like a pretty small thing, but it's the seed of an intentional life that's filled with meaning and purpose.

Sitting around and thinking about things is great, but of course, it's not the same as taking action. Taking action without deliberate intention is just meaningless – you'll just blow around in the winds of other people's intentions. But dwelling on your intentions without having a concrete way to realize them in the world is just as meaningless. Ideas are just ideas. Thoughts remain thoughts. Nothing changes.

The bridge between wanting something and actually achieving it is *action*. To cross a river from point A to Point B, you can build a bridge. But there are many ways to build that bridge, some ways better than others.

This is the topic for this chapter: how the stories we tell ourselves mediate our actions, and form that bridge between dream and reality.

Here's an example.

Let's imagine you would like to lose weight. As you set your intention each morning and keep asking yourself what you really want in life, the idea comes up over and over: you'd like to feel lighter and more at ease in your body. Great. But now what? If you're like millions of people, you might launch into a punishing "cleanse" or splurge on a gym membership you never use or binge and promise you'll start something on Monday.

But there's an element of mindlessness at work in solving problems this way. This is a bit like jumping into building a bridge before you have a blueprint, then building something that's all wrong and doesn't quite reach the other side. Perhaps you start an elaborate bridge and realize halfway that you should have been building a tunnel all along!

Instead, take a look at the *stories* that you're working with, i.e. the materials you're using to build the bridge from desire to reality. In our example, you might discover that you keep telling yourself the following story about your weight:

"Losing weight is hard (actually it's pretty much impossible) and I can only ever do it by going to extreme measures like getting surgery or developing an eating disorder. I'm just built fat and always will be out of control, and if I want to be skinny I'm going to have to suffer and hate every minute of it. At the end of the day, people have to choose whether they'll be fat and happy, or skinny and miserable, and that's just a fact."

It might seem ridiculous when spelled out like that, but most of us are carrying around versions of the above story, give or take a few details. We might have carried them around so long that we barely even notice that they're there anymore. We assume that we're just witnessing reality as it is. A "story" is made of our self-talk and all the things we tell ourselves about who we are, what we're capable of and why things happen. If you're not convinced that you have any stories of your own, just listen carefully and you're bound to notice them eventually – because the best stories are those that seem invisible at first!

Stories can take any form, but the more negative ones might look like this:

- "Sure, XYZ applies to other people, but not to me. I'm different/worse somehow."

- "There is something wrong with me, at my core, and so I'll never succeed, not really."

- "Changing is scary and not worth it. It's better to stick with what you know."

- "My happiness is out of my control anyway, so there's no point trying to do something about it."

Stories are tricky because they're wrapped into our identities, and built into the foundation of our lives. Our stories might be handed down to us from our parents or given to us by our cultures or those close to us. No matter how reasonable a story is, though, it's always just that: a story.

Let's return to our example. If you told yourself that weight loss was basically impossible and that trying to change automatically meant you'd have to be unhappy, what would happen? Well, maybe you'd go to gym for a week, and wake up very stiff one morning. In your story, trying to lose weight = pain. You feel uncomfortable. And according to your story, staying the same = happiness. Who wouldn't choose happiness over pain? It's obvious that if you've been telling yourself this story, the thing to do is give up on weight loss.

Except the problem is that your story was *a lie*. With this set of beliefs, even if you went to gym for a month and actually started to see some results, you'd look at those results through the lens of your story. *"All weight loss is only temporary and I had to sacrifice so much for such a little progress and anyway my genes are fat so I can never really change..."*

Remember that in this story, weight loss is impossible. A healthy lifestyle is painful and inconvenient. Fat is inevitable. So everything that doesn't fit that story is just pushed aside or ignored. Even success! According to the story, failure is a given. So even if you *don't* fail, you end up acting in a way that aligns with the story, rather than what you see out there in the world. It's easier to fail and stick to the story than change the story. You've built a bridge that will never carry you to where you want to go.

Story Exercise One: Learning to Listen Carefully

The only way to change a story that isn't working for you is to become aware it's even there in the first place. How do you become more aware of your own self-limiting beliefs? What stories are you carrying around with you, telling yourself over and over again? More importantly, are those stories helping you get closer to where you want to be or are they actually doing the opposite?

Well, there's no easy way around it: you have to listen!

Formal meditation is a great way of doing an inventory of everything that's swirling around in your mind. Instead of taking everything at face value, you can stop, become aware of what programming you're really running, and give yourself the chance to change it.

If you don't already meditate, well, it's easy to start. Simply find a quiet place to sit and pay attention to your breathing. That's all. You don't need to do anything fancy, just become aware. Focus on the sounds and sensations around you. Try to be aware of them without passing judgment. Turn that awareness inwards as well, and watch yourself in the same way.

What thoughts and emotions bubble up in you? Watch them from a distance instead of getting carried away with each passing change in your internal landscape. Notice what thoughts and feelings are most persistent – but remember, there's no judgment. Just become aware, then let it go. There is no way to do it wrong – just watch.

You don't have to wait till you're meditating to try and become aware, though. Carve out little moments during the day where you take a step back and breathe. What are you thinking? What are you feeling?

- Try wearing a bright band round your wrist. Every time you glance at it, pause and take a look at what "thought traffic" you're in the midst of.

- Take natural pauses during the day – on the hour, every time you go for a bathroom break or when it's time to eat. Notice your state of mind.

- During particularly emotional times, try to remember to stay aware. Your stories will come out in full force during stressful or upsetting moments, so pay attention if you can!

As you practice becoming more aware, note down some of the stories that come up again and again. Store them in a notebook somewhere, if you can.

Imagine a man who's having trouble dating. He is getting despondent, a never-ending stream of disappointing first dates and women who seem utterly uninterested in him. Instead of getting angry or forking over money for useless dating advice, he decides to try become more aware of the stories he's telling himself.

As he watches for a few months, he is soon shocked to discover a story he has been telling himself routinely for most of his life. Even though he never consciously realized it, this story was sabotaging his romantic life at every turn. The story goes: "I'm a complete loser, and I will never get a girl to be interested in me. Therefore, if a girl IS interested in me, there must be something wrong with her! I don't want a girl like that..."

Besides being untrue, this story had the same predictable result: when women were interested in him, they were immediately written off. After all, according to his story, only girls he didn't want wanted him, right? And in just the same way, his story told him that a girl who rejected him was actually the one he wanted. This story had him actively moving away from women who were interested in him and towards those who weren't. Exactly the opposite of what he wanted!

Story Exercise Two: Changing the Story

Digging down deep into your personal stories can be hard work – after all, stories are everything. They help us make sense of other people, the world and our place in it. The stories we tell are the very blueprints we build our lives on. Our stories tell us what is and isn't possible. That's why if you want to make lasting changes, it makes sense to start deep down on this level.

In this second exercise, let's take a look at those life blueprints. The key questions to ask is: what would life be like without the stories you tell yourself?

In our weight loss example, the story is clearly a limiting one. It's tricky because many people (advertisers included!) will go along with this story and encourage it. But is it really true that you have no choice but to suffer and be fat? How do you act and behave when you believe that meaningful change is impossible or unpleasant? Are you happy to act that way and is acting that way getting you the results you want in life?

Let's say the person in our example realizes the story they've been telling themselves is no good and only makes them apathetic. Because they've been practicing setting their intention and being more deliberate (the first principle), they actively decide to change this story to a more reasonable one:

"Losing weight is hard but more than possible, if I stay consistent. I'm always in control. I have made the decision to take care of myself and I'm willing to be a little uncomfortable while I adjust to a healthier, happier lifestyle. I give myself permission to go through the process."

In this story, weight loss and happiness are not set at odds; rather they are the same thing. Gone is the all-or-nothing, pessimistic thinking and instead this story acknowledges that changing takes time and occasional discomfort, but is completely possible.

Now, when such a person wakes up one morning feeling stiff from working out, they will look at the stiffness and say, "ah, this is all normal and part of the process. It's OK. I'll keep going." The story is in alignment with the ultimate goal. Change is welcomed and encouraged.

If you've written your stories down, take a look at them now and ask where you would be without them. Can you moderate them so that they're more in line with your goals? Look carefully and see how reading each of your stories makes you *feel*. Do you feel demotivated and demoralized? What changes could you make so that your stories energize you instead?

For example, if your story is "I've failed so much in my life, I'm a failure", how do you behave? How would your behavior change if the story was, "I have a chance to make each new day a success"? Would your eyes be open to new opportunities and would you be quicker to forgive yourself and focus on the future instead of the past?

Of course, you don't have to be ridiculous about making changes to your stories. You don't have to be unrealistic or overly optimistic. Neutral is just fine! The next time you catch yourself telling the same old story, deliberately step in and change it. You've taken a lifetime to develop those habits, so expect it to take a while to develop new ones. But in time, your story will change. And when your blueprint is different, your actions begin to change in alignment with it. Gradually, your life begins to shift and change shape.

- Look closely for absolute statements – these are clues that you're dealing with a story, i.e. "always", "never", "perfect", "nobody". You can often make a story less limiting merely by adjusting these extreme statements. Do you *always* fail? Really? Are you sure you don't just fail some of the time?

- Look for those statements that feel like they have the most emotional heft to them. This is a sign that you're deviating from objective reality and are in the realm of a story. "Everybody hates me" is not only emotionally painful, it's factually untrue. The more boring truth is that most people are indifferent! Look for emotive wording in the stories you tell yourself. Are you petrified or disgusting or a failure? Or are you busy adjusting and doing the best you can? The words you use matter.

- Change your stories to ones that inspire you to act. Take note which words, phrases, thoughts and beliefs leave you feeling calm, strong, level headed and ready to take meaningful action. That's the direction you should be headed. Get rid of those beliefs that immobilize you.

When you learn how to go in deep and change the stories that run your life, you make lasting, meaningful changes. If you sincerely believe that you are doomed to be overweight, no amount of well-meaning dieting or exercise advice is going to help. The problem is more fundamental than that.

But when you reach inside and become curious about the narrative you've spun for yourself, you open your eyes to new solutions and possibilities that were invisible to you before. Then, change becomes something real and possible for you. Your dreams and goals which seemed so far away before, come more sharply into focus. You realize that they were always there, within your grasp.

Chapter 5 - Learning to Add Value

Let's recap.

So far, we've been slowly building on three key principles for a meaningful, purpose-driven life. In the first chapter, we looked at becoming more aware and gradually tuning into that inner compass of our own desires. In the chapter after that, we expanded on those ideas and tried to see how those desires can be honed via the stories we tell ourselves.

In this chapter, we'll expand even further and look at how to bring those new, aligned stories to life with valuable action.

How do you know whether an action is valuable or not? How do you know when you're finished with your day or your week (or life, for that matter!) that you did a good job? Well, something is valuable when it aligns with your desires and goals. Your intention is the yardstick that you measure all your actions against – when you are aligned, you act with purpose and deliberateness, and so the things you do have innate value.

Hopefully by this point you've started to try and change some of your stories. It's challenging at first, but gradually you can begin to replace limiting stories with more valuable ones. The first two chapters might have seemed a little vague, and that's because nobody can really tell you what your values and goals are!

In this chapter, they can begin to crystallize and take shape. When you act in accordance with your newfound desires, your actions become those that enrich your life, rather than just eat time and have you asking, "what's the point?"

Value Exercise Number One: Value Yourself

As you looked close at your self-talk, did you find any stories that sound like the following?

- "I'm worthless."
- "I'm broken and can't be fixed."
- "I'm not rich/thin/young/happy enough to do X."
- "People are judging me. Nobody likes me and I'll never be loved and accepted."
- "I'm just an ordinary person, I can't do or be anything special."

Part of learning to identify and create a meaningful life is learning how to value yourself. When you think poorly of yourself, there's just no point in trying, or in pushing to fulfil your potential – why even bother if you don't have any potential?

This exercise comes in two parts. It might strike you as a bit contrived, but try it anyway: first, take 15 minutes or so to piece together a letter to your younger self. Imagine you have the ability to reach back in time and send a message to the 5-year-old version of yourself. Picture you as you were: young, innocent, full of hope, vulnerable, good.

How do you feel towards this child? Do you feel like saying, "you're broken and you can't be fixed" to this child's face? Does it seem right to tell them that nobody loves them and that they will never be accepted? Or are you filled with tenderness and a yearning to protect that younger self? Do you admire how that little person survived and grew and did what they could to navigate the sometimes cruel and unusual world around them? Are you fond of their spirit and their resilience and joy?

Take your time with this letter. Be honest. Try to see in this child all those things that make you who you are, even today. While it's true that you're an adult now and you are responsible for the choices you make, are you really so very different now compared to then? If you wouldn't say such negative things to child-you, why say them to adult-you?

The second part is to imagine yourself travelling forwards, not backwards to the past. Picture an older, wiser version of yourself. This is the person you are at 90 years old, after a lifetime of experience and insight and pain and joy. Now, take a few minutes to write the letter that your older self would write to you as you are now.

Would an older and wiser person tell you that they wished you had been harder on yourself, or that they regretted you didn't hate your body more? Do you think they would tell you that it was the right decision to hang back and never take any risks? Picture yourself on your death bed, your body tired and old. What would you wish your younger self had done, while there was still time? What is important? What isn't important?

A woman writes a letter to her younger self and in doing so, realizes that she wishes she had been given more encouragement for who she was as a child instead of pressured to be like everyone else. Perhaps she lived her whole life in the closet, forcing herself to be what she wasn't.

In writing a letter that tells her younger self not to be afraid of being different, she hears this message now, as an adult. When she writes the letter from her older, wiser self, the theme comes up again: she realizes that if she doesn't find the courage to express who she really is, she'll eventually regret it terribly. This exercise gives her the courage to finally come out of the closet.

These two exercises have a way of making all the bluster and distraction of everyday life shrink away and reveal what is ultimately important: that you are a human being, and that you deserve compassion and understanding. If you like, keep these letters and come back to them when you're stressing about something or feeling a little lost in life.

Value Exercise Number Two: Value Others

The life of an individual has meaning only insofar as it aids in making the life of every living thing nobler and more beautiful. Life is sacred, that is to say, it is the supreme value, to which all other values are subordinate.

Albert Einstein

Of course, a meaningful and fulfilling life is not just one where you feel smug about how wonderful you are. You can't just endlessly forgive yourself every mistake or spend your time navel-gazing.

There are other people in the world! And when you value them, you plug yourself into something bigger. The paradox is that sometimes, forgetting about your ego and the petty details of your own life can be incredibly liberating; loving others more can be a surprising route to loving yourself more. Finding meaning in others has a sneaky way of rubbing off, and helping you find meaning in yourself.

You can think of this exercise as a bit like an elaborate game of "devil's advocate". When people are hostile with one another, the root of their disagreement is usually a feeling that they are completely, irremediably *different* from each other. But for the most part, these differences are not innate things that keep people apart, but superficial differences that we ourselves have put there.

In fear, it's easy to look at another human being and find things that make him a threat to you. He looks different, speaks different, holds a different set of beliefs and has a different set of behaviors. But is he really that different from you?

For this exercise, forgo focusing on differences and instead focus on what makes you the *same* as the people you encounter. This switches your brain into a collaborative, receptive mode rather than a hostile and fearful one. It opens you up to possibilities instead of problems. It lets you honor your fellow human beings' innate dignity, rather than feeling intolerant that they aren't more like you. It lets you acknowledge that sometimes, *others* are right and that your convictions may actually not be so great.

So, when you are talking with someone new, before you do anything, immediately look for something in common with them. Perhaps they're standing in a long supermarket queue and are tired and fed up, just like you. Maybe they're the same age group as you, have toddlers like you or have a similar educational background.

This exercise works best when you feel that there's nothing in common at all. But look and you'll find something. Do you think the person in front of you has ever gone through a traumatic breakup and had to stop themselves from crying at work the next day? Do you think this person ever had an upsetting argument with a family member or has some sexual fantasy that they would never tell anyone for fear of being judged?

Once you start looking, you'll realize that the people you deal with every day, from close friends to strangers in the street, all have far more in common with you than not.

Take this a step further. Maybe this person is being rude and unkind to you. Maybe they are wrong about something and being completely unreasonable. Well, now you know you *definitely* have something in common with them – just look back into your past and remember all the times you yourself said something stupid or were unkind to someone. Does this make it easier to deal with them? Knowing that this person is not doing anything that you haven't done at one point yourself?

Value Exercise Number Three: Add Value to Everything You Do

When you ask people what their regrets are, they almost never say something like, "I wish I stayed longer in that soul-sucking job" or "I wish I was better at keeping up with my neighbors". Nobody looks back and wishes they toned things down a bit, or lived with a little less passion. And even if they look back and see the mistakes they made, they usually regret the things they *didn't* do rather than the things they tried but failed.

Once you start tuning into your intention, and once you become skilled at taking charge of your own story, everything you do becomes an opportunity to add value. When you are guided by a deeper purpose, all the noise and fuss of life has a way of disappearing into the background, and what's really important has a way of coming more clearly into focus.

For this exercise, start to think of how you can optimize on value, both the value you find in the world around you and in the value you *create* for yourself and others.

Throughout the day, stop to take a moment and become aware (luckily, you've been practicing this since the first chapter!). As you do an activity, ask, is this adding value to my life? As you engage with other people, ask yourself if they are guiding you closer or further away from the things you value. But don't stop there – ask if you are pulling you weight and doing everything you can to provide value to *them*.

Let go of people who are not truly present with you, who are working against what's important to you or using you for their own ends. At the same time, hold yourself to a high standard: are you giving all of yourself to the people you deal with, during every encounter? Are you being true to your word, compassionate, genuine? Or are you not even considering them at all?

When you constantly remind yourself to stay aligned to your values, and to *add* value, it's like gently nudging yourself closer and closer the path in life that will make you the most fulfilled. Instead of letting empty, mindless moments flit past you, never to return, you grab hold of them with decisiveness and fill them with things that are worth something. These little moments might not seem like much at the time, but they add up to a life that feels full and worthwhile.

Chapter 6 - Putting it All Together

If you're like me, you may have read some of the above and thought, "sure, I know all this already!" and then just skimmed through. But as we've seen, intellectually understanding an idea and actually *experiencing* it are two different things.

How can you take the three keys outlined above and actually use them, in the real life you live, right now, right here?

Unfortunately, our culture values quick fixes and secret tips and tricks that you can easily do once and then never again. We hope the three day cleanse will absolve us of a lifetime of poor eating habits or that reading one book once will somehow erase a lifetime of accumulated attitudes and beliefs that go against it.

But now that we've outlined three components to a life that is meaningful, intentional and free of regrets, let's look at practical ways to *live* that information.

- Instead of aiming for big changes, focus on making things habit. In just the same way as you engage in negative self-talk or mindlessness now out of habit, you can train yourself to do the opposite, just by sticking with it and reminding yourself to keep going each and every day. A morning ritual is the simplest and best way to do this. It's free, easy to do, and doesn't take much effort – yet it can make all the difference in the world. Set your intention, become aware, breathe and focus on your goals for the day and you learn to hit "refresh" on your life each and every morning.

- Let go of all or nothing thinking. "Perfectionism" is really fear of failure in disguise. But when you're OK with doing things wrong occasionally, you take more risks and try more things – and succeed more often. Give yourself permission to be a beginner, to not know everything and to be a little afraid. Any regretful person knows that the feeling of missed opportunity is so much worse than the temporary discomfort of going out of your comfort zone once in a while!

- Keep your motivation and locus of control *internal*. The moment you hand over power to an external authority, you take away meaning from your life. Do things because you *choose* to, not because you have to or should or because someone told you to. Even if you make a mistake, the fact that you have taken responsibility for your life and chosen that mistake autonomously gives you more freedom and purpose than doing the "right thing" without really thinking about it.

- Slow down. Mindlessness often comes with a kind of rushing in life. Stop, smell the roses, and take a moment for yourself. The answers to a problem often emerge when you stop grasping or looking for distractions to fill empty moments. Stop, feel just how full and rich each passing moment in time is, and give yourself time to really process what's happening around you.

- When you catch yourself comparing your life to other peoples', ask if that feeling is actually masking another, deeper feeling. Are there some desires going unfulfilled in you? Are you feeling guilty for not living up to potential you know you have? Instead of focusing on the people who elicit these reactions in you, ask what it is about you that's being "hooked" this way.

- When it comes to your own truth, don't be moderate. Speak up on matters that concern things of great importance to you. Today, apathy is often praised as a progressive, intelligent attitude – but don't be afraid to speak out. Many people regret not living more honestly, not fully expressing themselves, biting their tongues ...and then feeling hurt that nobody knows the "real" them. If you have the courage to express your true self, you give people the chance to relate to you in a deeper, more meaningful way – and you give other people the courage to do the same!

- Be wary of people or institutions who try to tell you what you think and feel. When others try to narrate your life for you or interpret your actions using their own stories, you become disempowered. Everyone from romantic partners to colleagues to advertisers and even to therapists can have unconscious agendas for squeezing you into stories that are meaningful to *them*. But are they meaningful to you? This is why it's so important to have space every single day to tune out the noise of daily life and go quiet enough to listen to your *own* voice.

- As you become more aware, more in control and more focused on a life geared to meaning, expect that things will start to change around you. You may be thrilled to find what new doors open, but be aware that many will *close*, too. A little compassion goes a long way when you realize that certain relationships, ideas or habits are no longer part of your journey anymore. Bid a good journey to the people who are not on the same path as you and go your own way. It may hurt to lose things and people that used to be important to you, but try to focus on the space that opens up for things and people that are better aligned with your values.

- Keep healthy. The exercises in this book, though simple, take a lot of effort and presence of mind to do each and every day. You simply won't manage if your body is tired, poorly nourished or buckling under stress or illness. Turn your awareness inward regularly to see what your body needs, and take care of yourself with enough sleep, good food and exercise.

- When you're feeling challenged or as though you're not making progress, that's your clue to have a closer look at your stories. Look closely at the thought that's distressing you. If you're telling yourself the story, "I should be progressing faster than I am now" you will cause yourself stress every time you pause or take a step back. But is that story really true? Is it helpful? Perhaps, instead of getting caught up in how you should be going faster, you can spend your efforts reworking your story. Is it really so bad to go at the speed you're going? Does rushing accomplish anything?

Chapter 7 - Last Words

In a way, I'm thankful for the regrets I've racked up so far. It's these regrets that have forced me to look more closely at my life and what I ultimately want to do with it. These days, when I feel that familiar sense of panic or unease when I'm in bed late at night and can't sleep, I take it as a sign that I've strayed a little from my path and need to stop, become aware and take charge again. I no longer fear this sense of dread but welcome it as a reminder that my time on this earth is limited, and that if I want a life of meaning and value, the time to do it is *now*.

Whenever I've engaged with the techniques and exercises I've shared here, whenever I've been fully present, intentional, compassionate and tuned towards adding value, I've found that it's actually *impossible* to feel any regret. How could I? In fact, when I can sustain these three key principles and find space for them in each and every day, my life overflows with meaning. The disappointments of life, the memories of painful things in the past, the losses all of us experience now and again and the senselessness of the world ...well, all of it is just so much easier to deal with.

I'm sharing these principles with you not because I think they are the be all and end all, but because they have been so useful in my own journey towards a life that really means something. If you are curious about what you're really capable of, I encourage you to push yourself. Give yourself permission to ask those dangerous questions and believe that your hopes and dreams are worth pursuing.

I don't know where your journey will take you, but I know for sure that if it's a meaningful journey, these three elements will feature in it, somewhere, somehow. If you wander off your path, trust that you'll find your way back to it if you just stop, be aware and learn to really listen to yourself. And if you face adversity, trust that you have everything you need within you to overcome it, if you can only grab hold of your own intention and stay true to your values.

Live *on purpose*.

Made in the USA
San Bernardino, CA
01 May 2017